Let's Celebrate

PRESIDENTS' DAY

BY Barbara deRubertis

ILLUSTRATED BY Thomas Sperling

D0813608

GEORGE WASHINGTON AND
ABRAHAM LINCOLN

The Kane Press • New York

For activities and resources for this book and
others in the HOLIDAYS & HEROES series, visit:
www.kanepress.com/holidays-and-heroes

Text copyright © 1992 by The Kane Press
Original illustrations on pages 1, 6, 7, 8, 9, 12, 22, 23 copyright © 1992 by The Kane Press
Photograph/image copyrights: cover (Washington) © Marcio Jose Bastos Silva/Shutterstock, cover (Lincoln) ©
dustin77a/Shutterstock; 3 (Washington) © Library of Congress, LC-DIG-pga-04159; 3 (Lincoln) © Library
of Congress, LC-DIG-ppmsca-19305; 4 © M. Taboubi; 5 © Bettmann/Corbis/AP Images; 7 © Library of
Congress, LC-DIG-pga-02997; 10–11 © Painting by Emanuel Gottlieb Leutze/The Metropolitan Museum
of Art, Image source: Art Resource, NY; 13 © North Wind Picture Archives via AP Images; 14 © Robert
Pernell/Shutterstock; 15 © SergiyN/Shutterstock; 16 © M. Taboubi; 17 © North Wind Picture Archives via
AP Images; 18 © NPS Photo; 19 © North Wind Picture Archives via AP Images; 20 © Library of Congress,
LC-USZC4-2472; 21 © Bettmann/Corbis/AP Images; 23 © Library of Congress, LC-USZC4-2777; 24 ©
Library of Congress, LC-USZC4-2439; 25 © Blue Lantern Studio/Corbis; 26 © Library of Congress, HAER
PA,1-GET.V,21—96; 27 © Library of Congress, LC-DIG-pga-03898; 28 © Library of Congress, LC-HS503-
2953; 29 © Steve Heap/Shutterstock; 30 © Galyna Andrushko/Shutterstock; 31 © Orhan Cam/Shutterstock;
32 © Alan Bailey/Shutterstock
All due diligence has been conducted in identifying copyright holders and obtaining permissions.

Library of Congress Cataloging-in-Publication Data

deRubertis, Barbara.
  Let's celebrate Presidents' Day : George Washington and Abraham Lincoln / by Barbara deRubertis ;
illustrated by Thomas Sperling. — Revised edition.
     pages cm. — (Holidays & heroes)
  ISBN 978-1-57565-649-6 (pbk. : alk. paper) — ISBN 978-1-57565-650-2 (e-book) — ISBN 978-1-
57565-726-4 (library reinforced binding edition : permanent paper)
  1. Presidents' Day—Juvenile literature. 2. Washington, George, 1732-1799—Juvenile literature. 3.
Lincoln, Abraham, 1809-1865—Juvenile literature. 4. Presidents—United States—Juvenile literature. I.
Sperling, Thomas, 1952- illustrator. II. Title. III. Title: Let us celebrate Presidents' Day.
  E176.8.D47 2014
  394.261—dc23
                                                2013037987

1 3 5 7 9 10 8 6 4 2

Revised edition first published in the United States of America in 2014 by Kane Press, Inc.
Printed in the United States of America

Book Design: Edward Miller
Photograph/Image Research: Maura Taboubi

Visit us online at **www.kanepress.com**.

 Like us on Facebook
facebook.com/kanepress

 Follow us on Twitter
@KanePress

We celebrate Presidents' Day every February by honoring our nation's presidents.

Two of our greatest American presidents were born in February. George Washington was born on February 22. Abraham Lincoln was born on February 12.

Presidents' Day always falls between these two important birthdays, on the third Monday of the month.

George Washington
Born on February 22, 1732

Abraham (Abe) Lincoln
Born on February 12, 1809

George Washington was born on February 22, 1732, in the British colony of Virginia.

At that time, there was no country called the United States of America. There were twelve American colonies that belonged to Great Britain. One more colony was added after George was born, making a total of thirteen.

The thirteen original colonies

New Hampshire

Claimed by both New York and New Hampshire

Massachusetts

New York

Rhode Island
Connecticut

Pennsylvania

New Jersey

Delaware

Maryland

Virginia

North Carolina

South Carolina

Georgia

Young George and his father at Ferry Farm

George's family moved to Ferry Farm when he was six years old. There he loved to ride horseback over the hills and fields.

George went to school as often as he could. But he usually did lessons at home, as most children did at that time. He liked math best.

He also learned from adults around him. George liked to learn by watching and listening.

When George was
eleven years old, his father died.

After this, he spent much of his time with
his brother Lawrence, who was fourteen years
older than George. Lawrence lived on a farm
he had named Mount Vernon.

Lawrence helped George improve his mind
and his manners. He was a hero to George.

With Lawrence's help, George learned to be a surveyor. At age sixteen, he was given his first job: exploring and mapping the Virginia frontier.

When George was twenty, Lawrence died. This was a sad time for George. He decided to leave Mount Vernon.

Eager for adventure, George joined Virginia's army. By the time he left the army six years later, he had become commander of the troops.

At age twenty-six, George married
Martha Custis, a young widow with
two children.

Martha was very
wealthy. For her
wedding, she wore
a yellow silk dress,
purple satin shoes,
and pearls in
her hair!
George was
handsome
in his blue
jacket lined
with red silk.

Washington returned to Mount Vernon with
his new family. He read all the latest books on
farming. George liked trying new ideas.

The Washingtons spent sixteen peaceful
years at Mount Vernon.

But trouble was on its way. People in the American colonies did not think they were being treated fairly by the British.

A meeting was called to discuss the problem. Washington watched and listened.

When he arrived at the second meeting, Washington was wearing his old army uniform. Everyone knew what that meant. Washington thought the time had come to fight for freedom from the British.

Washington was asked to lead the American army. He accepted the job, but he refused to accept any pay!

On July 4, 1776, the United States of America adopted its Declaration of Independence and claimed freedom from Great Britain.

The Revolutionary War followed. For a while, it looked as if the British would win.

Washington Crossing the Delaware, painted by Emanuel Leutze

But General Washington was clever and determined. A British general called him "the old fox." Once, Washington organized a surprise attack on Christmas night. He led his soldiers across the Delaware River in dark, cold weather and won an important victory.

The war lasted for eight years. In 1784, the the United States and Great Britain made peace.

At last, the American people had won freedom for their country.

After the war, Washington left the army and returned to Mount Vernon. For five years, he was happy just to be a farmer.

Then, once again, Washington was asked to help his country. The United States of America needed a president! Everyone thought Washington would do a good job.

Although he was content at Mount Vernon, Washington answered the call to serve his country.

George Washington was elected as our first president in 1789.

There were many problems facing the new country. President Washington tried to do what was right, even when it was not easy. He worked hard to make the country strong.

George Washington is sworn in as the first president of the United States

Washington enjoyed planning a new capital city. He chose a site on the Potomac River, across from Mount Vernon. The city was later named "Washington" in his honor.

After his second term as president, Washington returned home to Mount Vernon for the last time. Two years later, on December 14, 1799, he died.

Henry Lee, a longtime friend of George Washington, spoke at the memorial service. Fourteen words of Lee's tribute to Washington have become famous: "First in war, first in peace, and first in the hearts of his countrymen."

Above: A statue of George Washington in Westerly, Rhode Island

Opposite: The Washington Monument in Washington, D.C.

In another tribute, the minister Richard Allen recalled Washington's advice: "to love your country, to obey its laws, to seek its peace."

Many years later, in 1885, the towering Washington Monument was dedicated to the memory of our first president.

We remember George Washington on Presidents' Day.
He worked to make our country free and strong.

For this, we celebrate him.

Ten years after George Washington died, **Abraham Lincoln** was born.

The United States of America was facing new problems. These problems were growing more and more serious. Another clear-thinking and courageous leader would be needed.

Fortunately, Abraham Lincoln would be ready for the challenge.

The United States of America in 1809, the year Abraham Lincoln was born

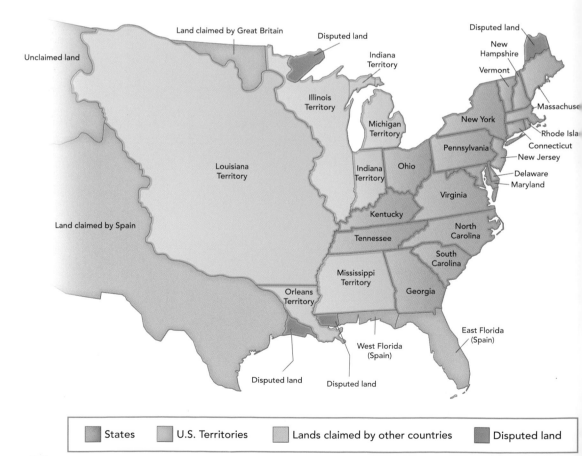

Young Abe Lincoln cutting wood for his mother

Abraham Lincoln was born in the state of Kentucky on February 12, 1809.

Abe and his family lived in a small cabin with one window and a dirt floor. Even as children, Abe and his older sister, Sarah, worked hard helping their parents. Abe's father taught him to chop wood as soon as he could lift the heavy ax.

The Lincoln family moved to Indiana when Abe was seven. Two years later, his mother died. It was a sad time.

The next year, Abe's father married a widow with three children. Abe's stepmother gave her new children, Abe and Sarah, as much love as her own. She made a cozy, cheerful home for everyone. Years later, Abe spoke of her as his "angel mother."

Lincoln Boyhood National Memorial, Indiana. This is a replica of Abe's Indiana childhood home.

Abe was happy
when he was able
to go to school.
Because all the
children said
their lessons
aloud at the
same time, it
was called the
"blab" school.

But Abe was
not able to attend school often. In farm areas,
teachers had to travel around to many different
schools. Sometimes school would last for just a
few weeks.

However, Abe learned in other ways. He
loved reading. As Abe grew up, he used every
spare minute to read. He would walk many
miles just to borrow a book. One of his favorite
books was about George Washington!

Above: Abe Lincoln as a boy, reading by firelight in his family's cabin

Abe continued to help his parents as much as he could. He also worked for other settlers, clearing fields and splitting logs for fences.

Abe enjoyed going to the general store in town. He could read newspapers there and listen to people talk. Abe was good at telling jokes and stories. The shopkeeper gave him a job because people liked him.

One day, the shopkeeper asked young
Lincoln to take some goods down the river to
New Orleans. There he saw people being sold
as slaves. He thought this was terribly wrong.
He never forgot what he saw.

When Lincoln returned home, he had to quit
his job and help his family move to Illinois. He
soon found a new job at a store there.

At the store, Lincoln made a lucky discovery. He found a law book stored in an old barrel. Lincoln had always wanted to study law. He dusted off the book and began to read.

After studying many books, Lincoln passed the law exam. Now he could be a lawyer! Meanwhile, friends had asked Lincoln to run in a state election. The first time he ran, he did not get enough votes. He lost. But the second time he ran, he won!

When he was thirty, Lincoln fell in love with Mary Todd. Two years later, they were married. The Lincolns had four sons, named Robert, Edward, William, and Thomas.

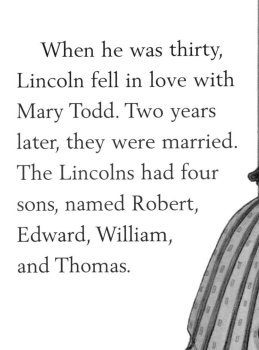

Lincoln and his son Thomas ("Tad")

Abraham Lincoln, congressman-elect from Illinois

In 1846, Lincoln was elected to Congress. There he spoke out against slavery. He believed that *no one* had the right to make another person a slave.

Next, Lincoln ran in an election for the Senate. His many speeches about slavery made him famous. Lincoln lost the election, but he was not ready to give up.

He would run for president!

In 1860, Abraham Lincoln was elected as the sixteenth president of the United States. But there was no time for celebrating. The arguments about slavery were tearing the country apart.

A group of southern states withdrew from the United States. They formed a separate country called the Confederate States of America. Soon, the North and the South were at war with each other.

Gettysburg National Military Park, site of the Battle of Gettysburg in 1863

Lincoln wanted to keep the United States together. He was willing to see a war fought if it would keep his country from breaking apart.

Finally, after four years, the Civil War ended. The North and the South were back together as one country. The United States of America was "united" again.

Now Lincoln could end slavery! He knew he had the support of many Americans. But he also knew there were people who hated him enough to kill him.

Five days after the war's end, President and Mrs. Lincoln went to a theatre. During the play, a man sneaked up behind Lincoln and shot him. The President died the next day, on April 5, 1865.

Later that same year, a law was passed that ended slavery in the United States. For the first time, *all* people of our country were free.

Lincoln's dream had finally come true.

"Emancipation"
Lincoln's dream to end slavery came to pass on December 6, 1865, with the 13th Amendment to the Constitution.

In 1922, the Lincoln Memorial was dedicated in Washington, D.C. Inside this beautiful building rests a famous statue of Abraham Lincoln.

Chiseled in one wall of the memorial is Lincoln's Gettysburg Address. In this speech, he spoke of his hope that the nation "shall have a new birth of freedom, and that government of the people, by the people, for the people, shall not perish from the earth."

Statue of Abraham Lincoln inside the Lincoln Memorial

Sunrise behind the Washington Monument, as seen from inside the Lincoln Memorial

*We remember Abraham Lincoln
on Presidents' Day.
He worked to make all people in
our country free.*

For this, we celebrate him.

The Mount Rushmore National Memorial in South Dakota bears the faces of four U.S. presidents: George Washington, Thomas Jefferson, Theodore Roosevelt, and Abraham Lincoln.

When we celebrate Presidents' Day every February, we remember all the presidents who have served our country.

We remember the times they tried to do what was right, even when it was not easy.

*We remember all our presidents
on Presidents' Day.
They worked to protect our country and
our freedoms.*

For this, we celebrate them.

The White House in Washington, D.C., has been the official home of the president of the United States since the year 1800.

Voting for a new president every four years is a big responsibility.

We are grateful to our voters for trying to choose good presidents.

We honor America's voters
on Presidents' Day.
They try to choose good leaders.
And by voting, they help to
protect our country's freedom.

For this, we thank them!